Hover & Soar

By

Stanley R. Taylor

Printed by Lighting Source Inc., Ingram Book Group, U.S.A.
Published by Stanley R. Taylor
Published in Canada

Published by Stanley R. Taylor
PO Box 137
Leaskdale, ON, Canada
L0C 1C0

Email: stanscienceman747@gmail.com

ISBN: 978-0-9918098-3-7

Edited by Bobbi Beatty, Silver Scroll Services
Front cover design by Bridget O'Connor, Illustrator

Contents

This book is dedicated to all children with whom I have had the privilege of building balloon-powered hovercrafts and simple balsa wood gliders with control surfaces.

Introduction

Some vocabulary descriptions are necessary to understand the concepts taught in this book.

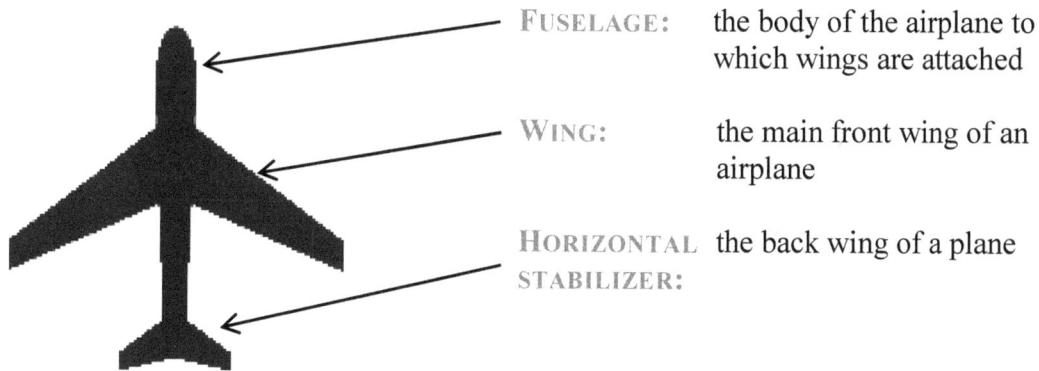

FUSELAGE: the body of the airplane to which wings are attached

WING: the main front wing of an airplane

HORIZONTAL STABILIZER: the back wing of a plane

FIG. 0.1

VERTICAL STABILIZER: the tail of the plane

FIG 0.2

Ailerons allow a plane to bank (roll slightly) or roll upside down to right side up.

To roll the plane to the right or left, the ailerons are raised on one wing and lowered on the other. The air hits the raised aileron causing it to drop. When one aileron is up, the other automatically goes down. If the left aileron is up, the plane rolls to the left as shown in Figure 0.3.

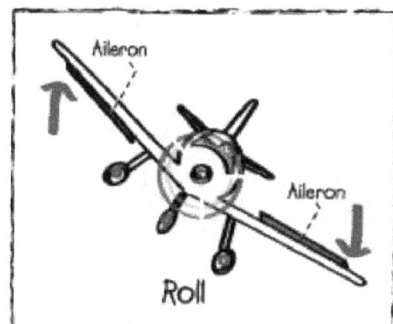

FIG 0.3

The elevators control the pitch (up or down motion) of the airplane (Fig. 0.4).

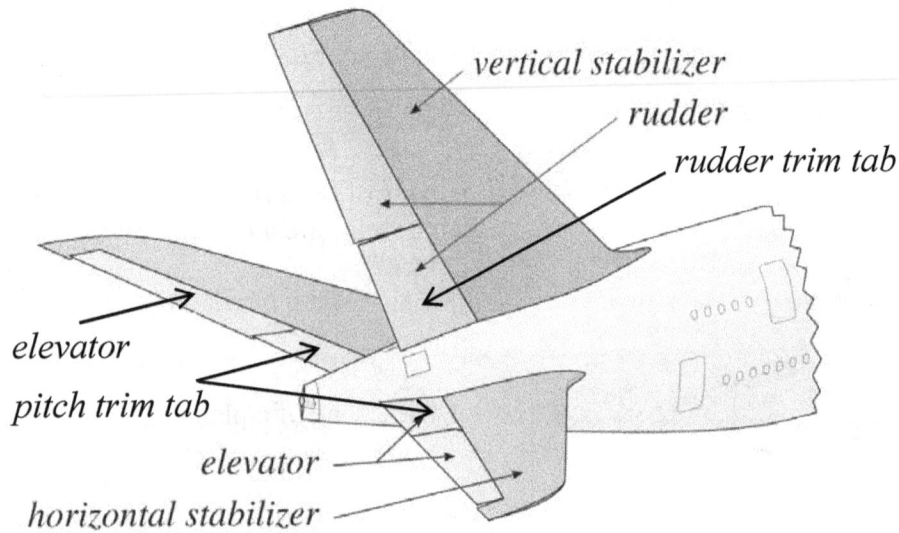

FIG. 0.4 (AIRBUS A380, *WIKIPEDIA*)

Pitch makes a plane descend or climb. When both elevators are up, the air hits them, pushing the tail down and causing the nose (front of the plane) to rise. If both elevators are down, the air causes the tail to rise and the nose goes down.

Yaw is the turning of a plane. When the rudder is turned to the left, the air pushes the tail to the right, causing the nose to turn to the left. If the rudder points to the right, the plane turns to the right.

On delta wing planes, there are two options:

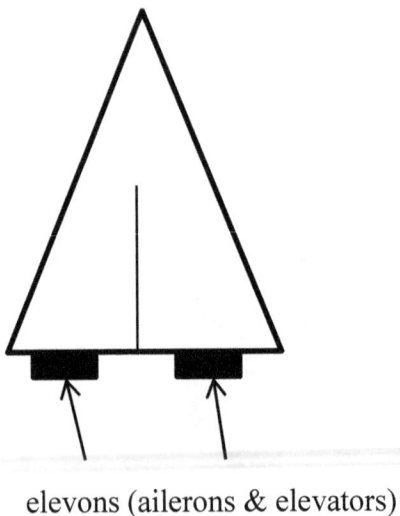

elevons (ailerons & elevators)
FIG. 0.5

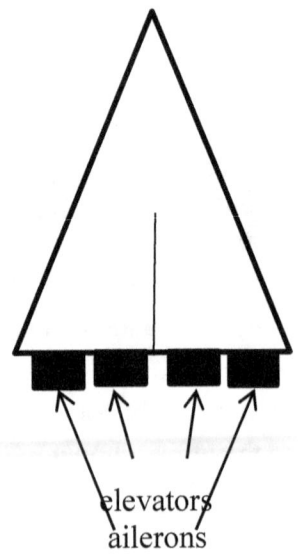

elevators
ailerons
FIG. 0.6

Laminar flow is the smooth flow over the wing with no turbulence.

A streamline is a path traced out by a massless particle moving with the flow.

A canard allows planes to fly more smoothly with less turbulence. The only drawback with a canard is that it reduces maneuverability of the aircraft.

Angle of Attack is the angle at which the wing attacks the air. On commercial airplanes it is 5 to 8° above the horizon.

Chapter 1 – Balloon Hovercraft

I am not certain how I got started making balloon-powered hovercrafts. I think it started in 2001 as I was trying to design an extension to the Grade 6 *Air and Flight* curriculum of 1998. Regardless of my uncertainty of origin, young children are delighted when I push my hovercraft across a table. After all, who does not like to play with a balloon?

Using the materials listed, make a hovercraft and try to make it travel as far as possible.

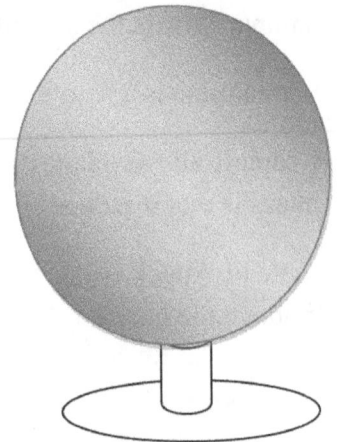

FRONT VIEW
FIG. 1.1

MATERIALS:

- 1 used CD

- 1 wooden spool from Stockade Wood Supply in Guelph, Ontario

- 1 – 12" party balloon

- 20 cm × 2 cm piece of duct tape

- thin card (if needed)

CONSTRUCTION:

1.   Tear the duct tape into 4 pieces about the same length.

2.   Centre the spool over the hole of the CD.

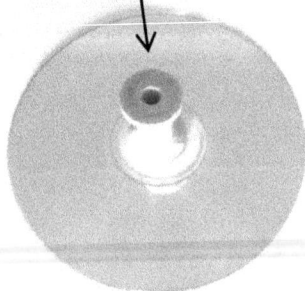

TOP VIEW
FIG. 1.2

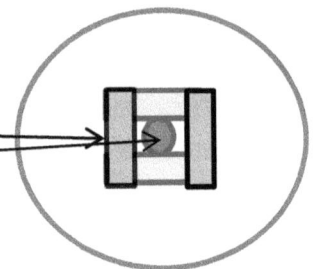

FIG. 1.3

Hover & Soar

3.	Take 1 piece of tape and attach half of it lengthwise to the base of the spool and the other half onto the CD (Fig. 1.5). Take another piece of tape and tape it on the opposite side of the spool (Fig. 1.5). Take the third piece and tape it 90° to the first piece. Tape the fourth piece opposite the third piece (Fig. 1.6).

FIG. 1.5   FIG. 1.6   FIG. 1.7

4.	Inflate the balloon to stretch it somewhat. Let the air out. Attach it over the wooden spool (Fig. 1.7).

TESTING:

1.	Inflate the balloon by blowing through the base of the CD.

2.	Gently push it along a smooth surface.

How far did it go in cm (m)?

Objective: To demonstrate Newton's First and Third Laws of Motion. Air coming out of the balloon in a downward motion is the action and the CD rising is the reaction (Third Law: for every action there is an opposite reaction). The distance the disc travels is related to thrust and friction (First Law).

Objective: To demonstrate Newton's First Law—a body at rest will remain at rest unless some force acts upon it. A body in motion will remain in a straight line motion unless some force acts upon it (Pushing the hovercraft is the force from rest to motion. The slowing down of the hovercraft is due to friction and the deflating of the balloon.).

EXTENSION:

1.   How can you make the balloon cover a greater distance?
(Possible answers: Use larger balloons, use smoother surfaces,
cut a straw the length of the spool and put it inside to make the
hole narrower and possibly increase the force of the thrust).
Experiment with different surfaces, e.g., sandpaper, rubber,
acrylic, cork, polished and lacquered pine. Do they have any
effect on slowing the hovercraft?

2.   How can you prevent the balloon from dragging
behind once its air is expended? (Possible answer: Place a thin
card [20 lb. card stock] around the neck of the balloon to
elevate the upper part of the balloon when the air is expended to
prevent it from dragging behind the disc and onto the surface.)

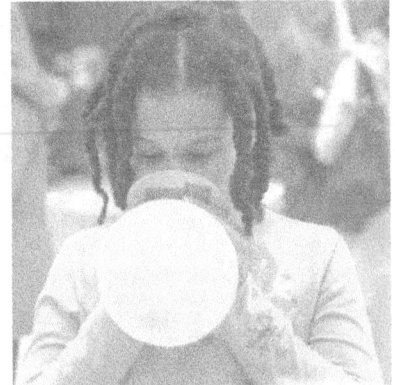

FIG. 1.8 A student inflating
her balloon-powered
hovercraft

3.   Have a contest.

(a)   Get a piece of pine 1.75 cm (½") thick by 20 cm (8") wide by 90 cm (3') long
and sand it to make the surface smooth.

(b)   Get 2 – 25 cm (4") Ardox nails and nail them into one side of the wood 2.5 cm
(1") from each side and 40 cm (16") from the end.

(c)   Attach a wide rubber band over each nail.

(d)   Place a mark of the board 10 cm (4") from the edge the nails are closest to.

(e)   Put the hovercraft on the board with the balloon inflated, and have the
hovercraft's maker pinch the bottom of the balloon above the spool to stop air leakage.

(f)   Back the wooden spool part of the hovercraft onto the rubber band and pull it
back 30 cm (12") to the mark on the board.

(g)   At the count of 3, release the spool and the squeezed balloon at the same time.

(h)   Measure the distance.

(i)   Depending on the size of the group and your budget, have more than one board.

Discuss possible variables of this method of testing hovercrafts for distance and ways to control
the variables.

Chapter 2 – Paper Towel Roll Balsa Wood Gliders

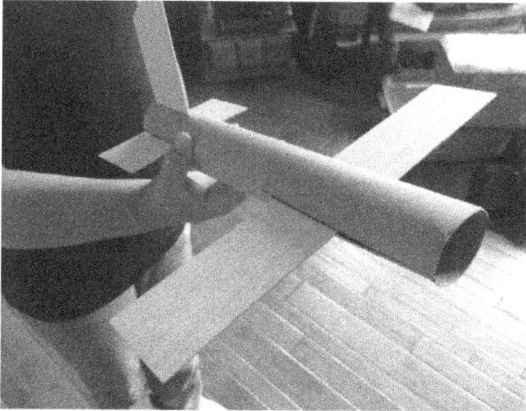

FIG. 2.1 Paper towel roll balsa wood glider

I first designed these gliders for a workshop I did in Toronto for deaf children at their annual picnic in 2005. I chose paper towel rolls because it would be easier to line up the parts of the glider when assembling it. I repeated this workshop for educators at the Science Teachers Association of Ontario annual conference in 2015. Paper towel or toilet paper rolls make the least expensive planes. Buy $1/16$" balsa wood. You can easily cut it with a pair of scissors. Put the wing on the end of the roll in the middle horizontally and mark the edges of the roll with a marker (Figs 2.2, 2.4). Draw a horizontal line along each side twice as long as the width of the wing (Fig. 2.3, 2.5). Cut along each line (Fig. 2.6).

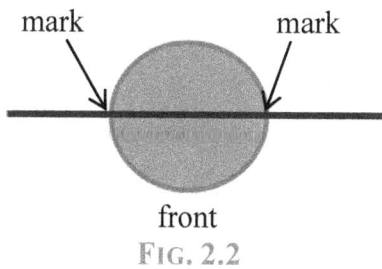
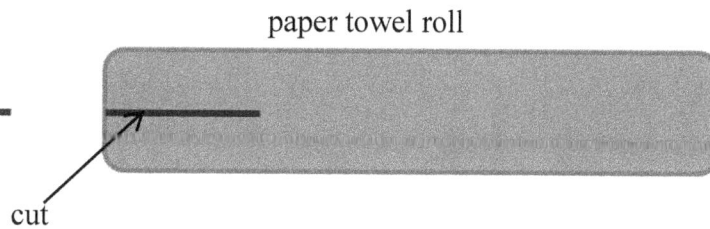

FIG. 2.2

FIG. 2.3

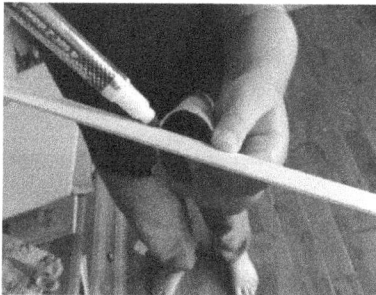
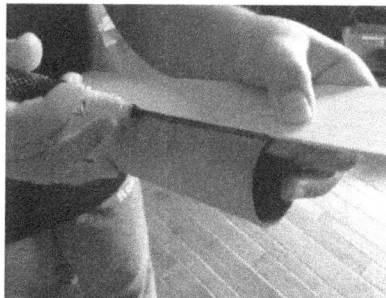
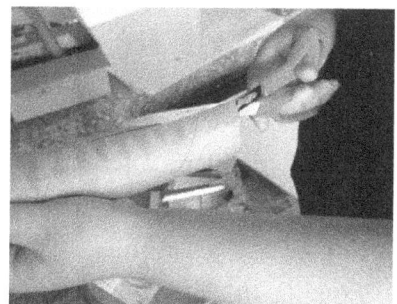

FIG. 2.4 marking wing on tube end   FIG. 2.5 drawing line   FIG. 2.6 cutting along the line

Slide the wing in along the two cuts.

Repeat the process for the other end of the roll, except make the line about 1.5 times the width of the horizontal stabilizer (rear wing). Cut another line at 90° of the horizontal stabilizer lines to accommodate the vertical stabilizer. Put a piece of two-way (two-sided) sticky tape on the centre of the horizontal stabilizer. Attach the vertical stabilizer (tail) to the tape (Fig 2.9).

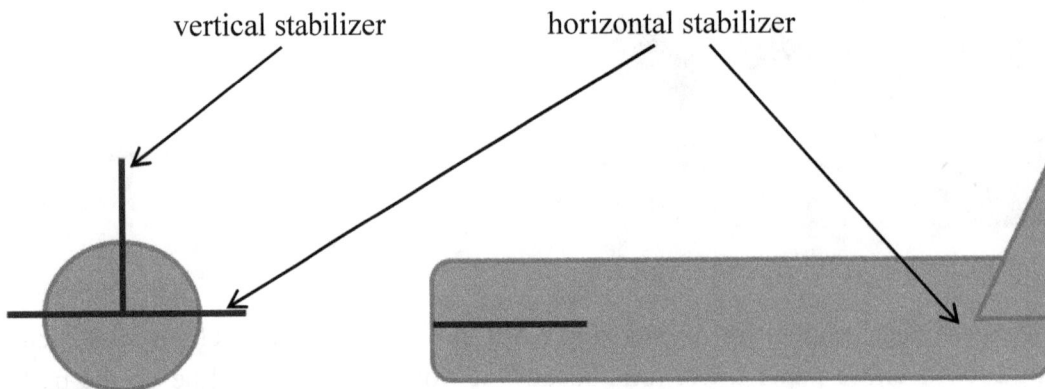

FIG. 2.7   FIG. 2.8

   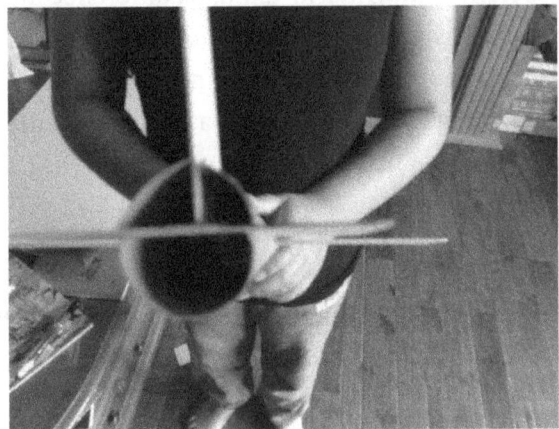

FIG. 2.9   FIG. 2.10

Slide the horizontal stabilizer and vertical stabilizer into the rear of the tube along the three cuts (Fig. 2.10).

Throw the plane a few times to see how it flies. If the nose goes up then the glider just falls, it is too light. Fasten a large paper clip on the bottom front and a small paperclip on the bottom back. Secure the paperclips with duct tape. **SAFETY**: Insure all students are wearing safety glasses. Practice one or two more flights following the directions of the instructor.

FRONT VIEW OF A PLANE WITH AILERONS – When one aileron is up, the other is down. The air hits the aileron that is up, pushing that wing section down causing the plane to roll (Figs. 2.11, 2.12).

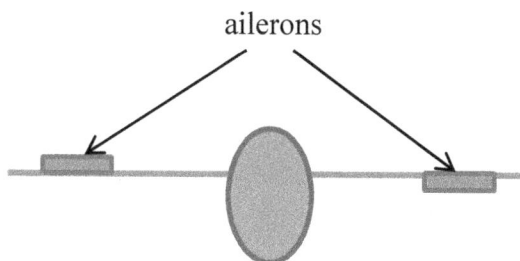

ailerons

FIG. 2.11

FIG. 2.12

BACK VIEW OF A PLANE WITH ELEVATORS – Both elevators are either up or down. The air hits the elevators when they are up pushing the tail down, causing the nose to rise. The nose up or down motion is called pitch.

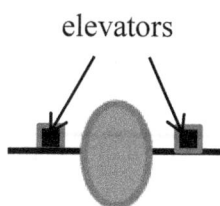

elevators

FIG. 2.13

SIDE VIEW OF THE PLANE WITH RUDDER

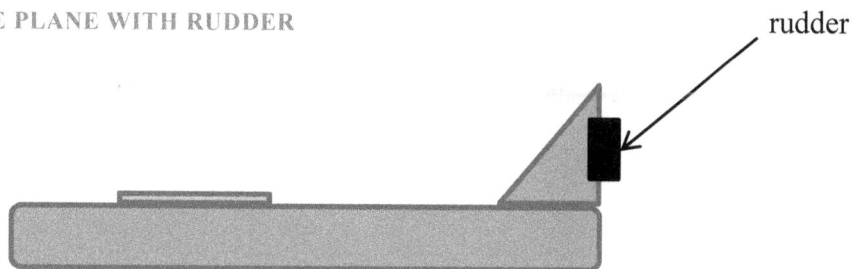

rudder

FIG. 2.14

When the rudder moves to the left, the air hits it, causing the vertical stabilizer to move to the right and causing the nose to move to the left. The left and right motion of a plane is called yaw.

SAFETY: Insure all students are wearing safety glasses. Practice one or two flights following the directions of the instructor.

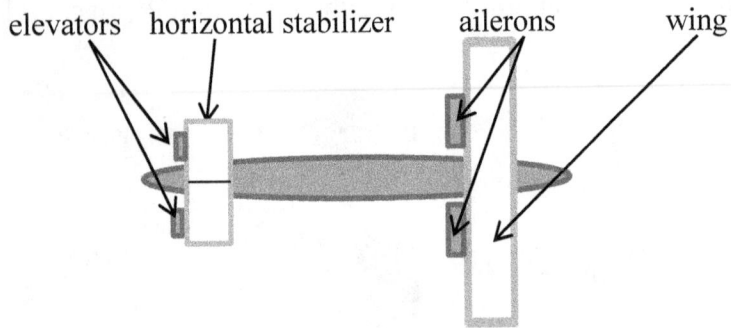

FIG. 2.15 TOP VIEW

FIG. 2.16 SIDE VIEW

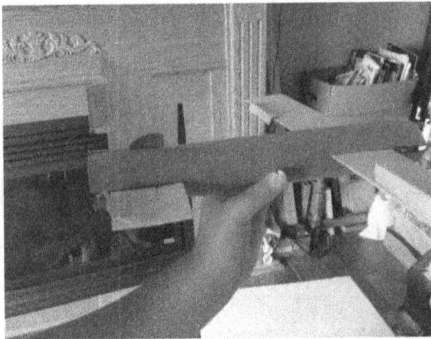

FIG. 2.17

If the plane banks left or right, try centering the wing more accurately. If dives into the floor, it is nose heavy. Add a paper clip to the rear of the roll. Hold it in place with duct tape. If it moves up then falls or just doesn't fly, it is tail heavy or it is too light and needs more weight. Add a paper clip to the front of the roll. Hold it in place with duct tape. If it is still too light, add small pieces of plasticine just behind the wing so that the plane balances (centre of gravity), and secure them with duct tape. Figure 2.17 shows the ailerons, elevators, and rudder attached to the glider.

Chapter 3 – Straight Wing Balsa Wood Gliders

When I taught Grade 6 at St. Barnabas School in Scarborough in 1998, I had my students build a balsa wood glider to scale. Using grid paper (Appendix A), they would use a scale of 1:1 to start with (later other scales were introduced) and draw top, front, and side views of the plane they wanted to design. I previously taught them how to draw items from these three perspectives using blocks of wood. The students would submit their designs to two other students who I put in charge of handling and cutting the wood. My two wood handlers would cut out the fuselage, wing, and horizontal and vertical stabilizers exactly to the specifications given to them by the students' drawings. The cutting was done on a junior mitre box (about half the size of the one that carpenters use). The mitre box uses a hacksaw with a very fine-toothed blade to cut the wood. I found that the hacksaw does not tear the balsa wood like a saw with larger teeth would.

This is an exercise in organized chaos. Some students are designing, some are having their design pieces cut; and some are assembling and gluing the various parts into place. I had my students fly their planes one at a time down the hallway. The students had many interesting designs. All of their planes flew. It was a great experience.

The band saw in my son-in-law's shop allows me to cut several pieces of wood at a time when I do community workshops. Classroom teachers do not have to precut the wood. That is what the students you assign to this task can do.

I bought my balsa wood (for the wings and tail) and basswood at a hobby store. Ask for a discount. Owners usually give one if it is for educational purposes.

I have taught children to make my balsa wood gliders at the following venues:

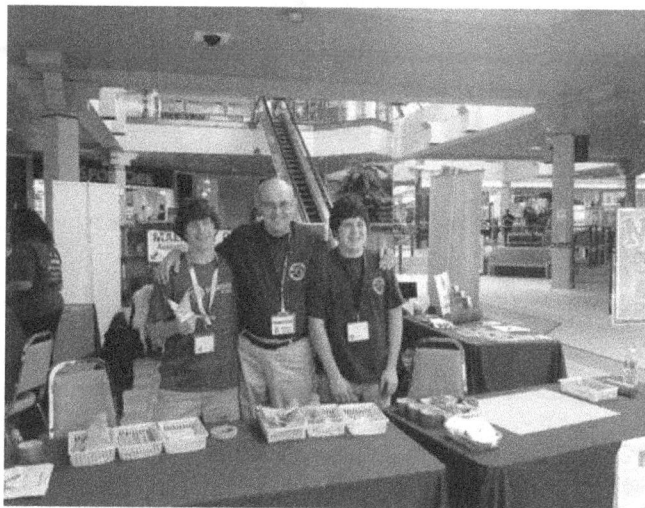

FIG. 3.1   With my fraternal twin grandsons Jakob and Nickolas in the Malls of Science for Science Rendezvous.

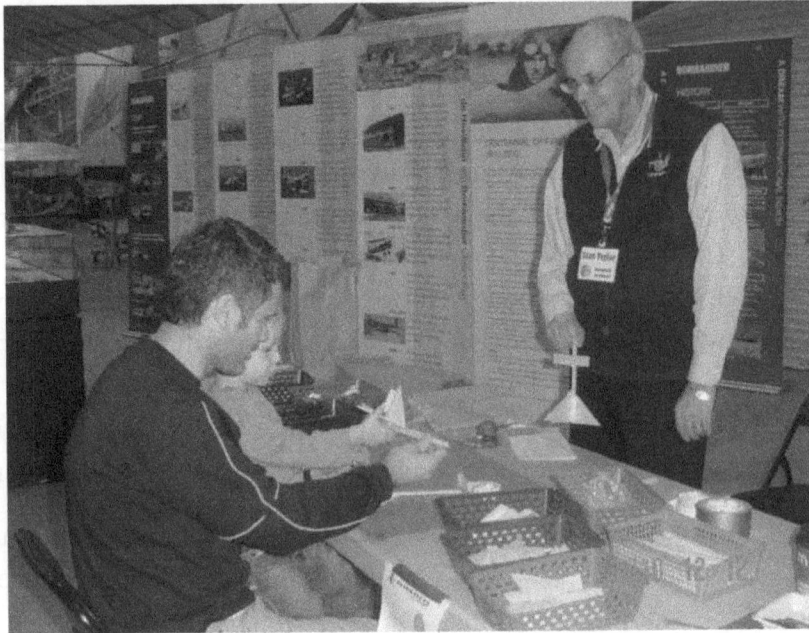

FIG. 3.2   At the Canadian Air and Space Museum at Downsview.

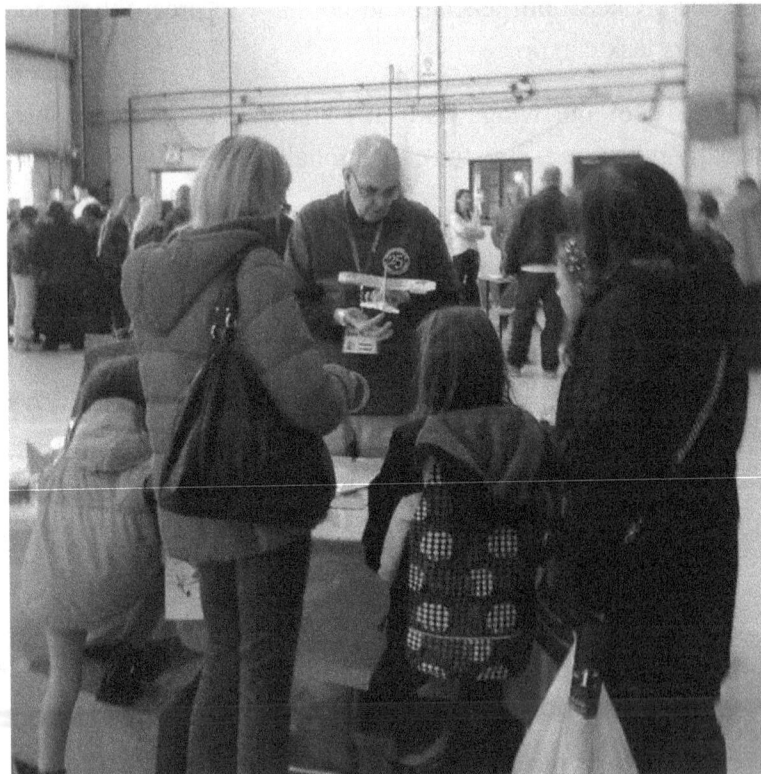

FIG. 3.3   At the Oshawa Airport's Women of Aviation World
Wide Week, Canadian 99s, and Durham Flight Centre.

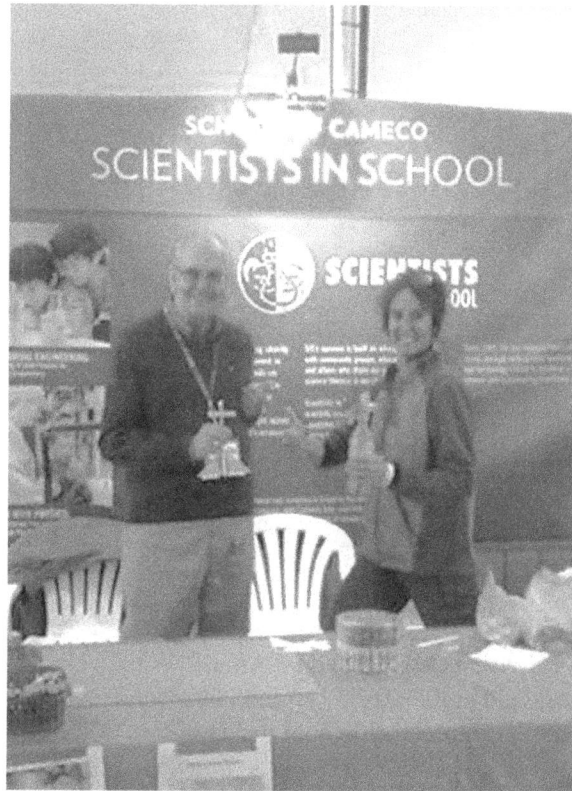

FIG. 3.4   During Engineering Week with Cameco (one of Scientists in School's [SiS] sponsors) at the Port Hope Fall Fair. To my left is Angela Maclean, a former presenter with SiS and now a school teacher with the Peterborough Victoria Northumberland and Clarington Catholic District School Board.

FIG. 3.5   With Ray Bielecki's AstroNut Kids Space Club in Newmarket.

FIG. 3.6   With Ray Bielecki's 5th and 6th Annual What's Up in Space Camp and STEM Contest held at the David Dunlop Observatory in Richmond Hill, ON, and Unionville Montessori School in Markham, ON, respectively.

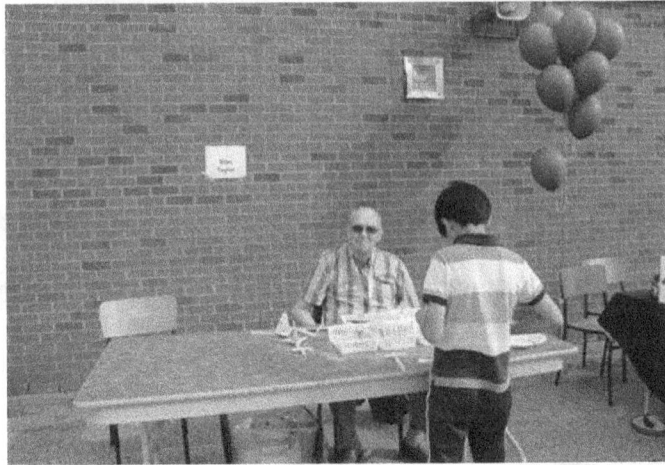

FIG. 3.7   With parents and their children at Blessed Scalabrini Catholic School Fund Raiser for the 2016-2017 school year's many special events.

FIG. 3.8 At the Oshawa Executive Airport Open House.

FIG. 3.9 At the Maine Space Day in Brunswick, Maine.

Chapter 4 – First Balsa Wood Glider

Designed by Stan Taylor

April 19, 1998

6 cm

FRONT VIEW

22 cm

0.5 cm

4 cm

1-3 cm

2.5 cm

2.5 cm

10 cm

TOP VIEW

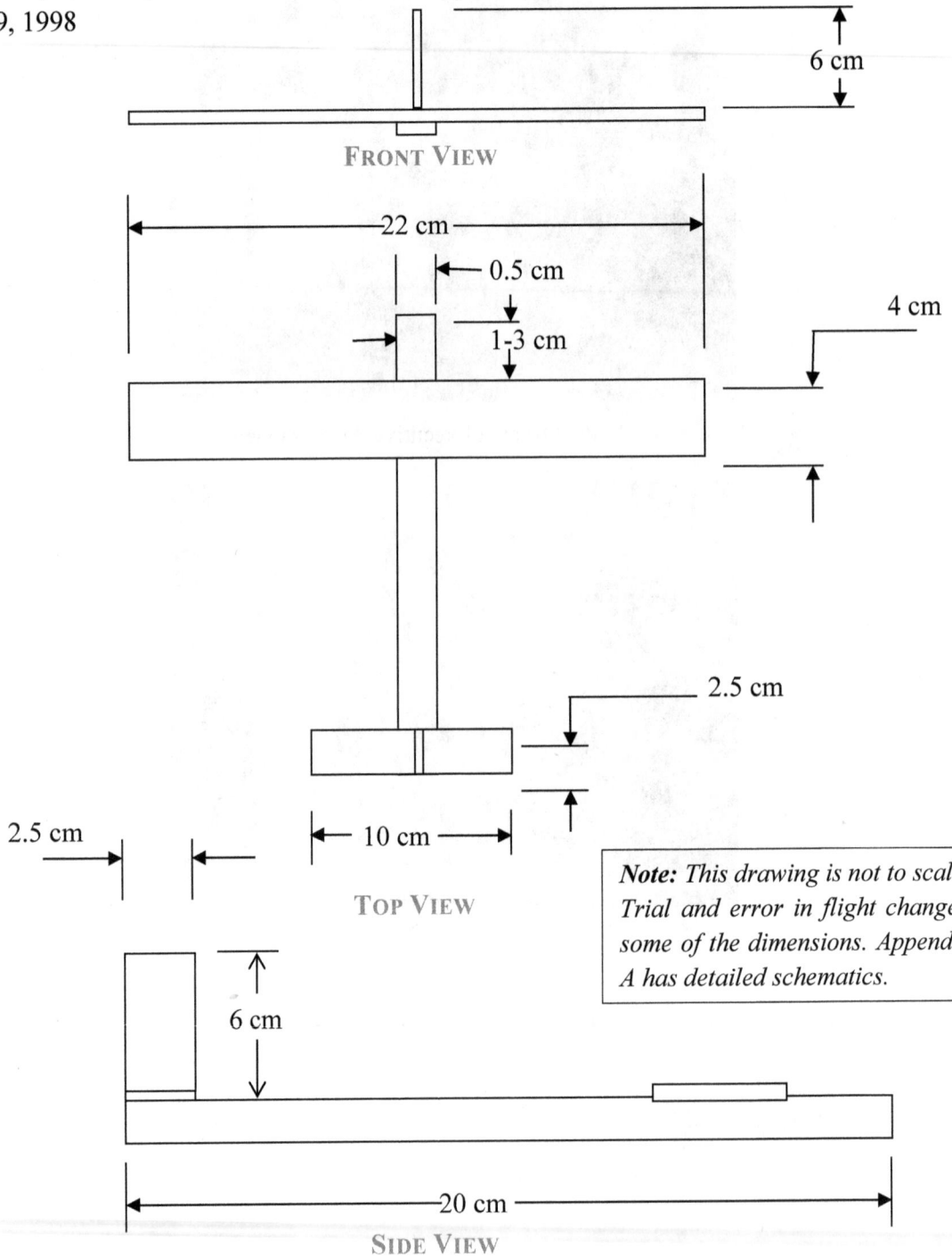

Note: This drawing is not to scale. Trial and error in flight changed some of the dimensions. Appendix A has detailed schematics.

6 cm

20 cm

SIDE VIEW

FIG. 4.1

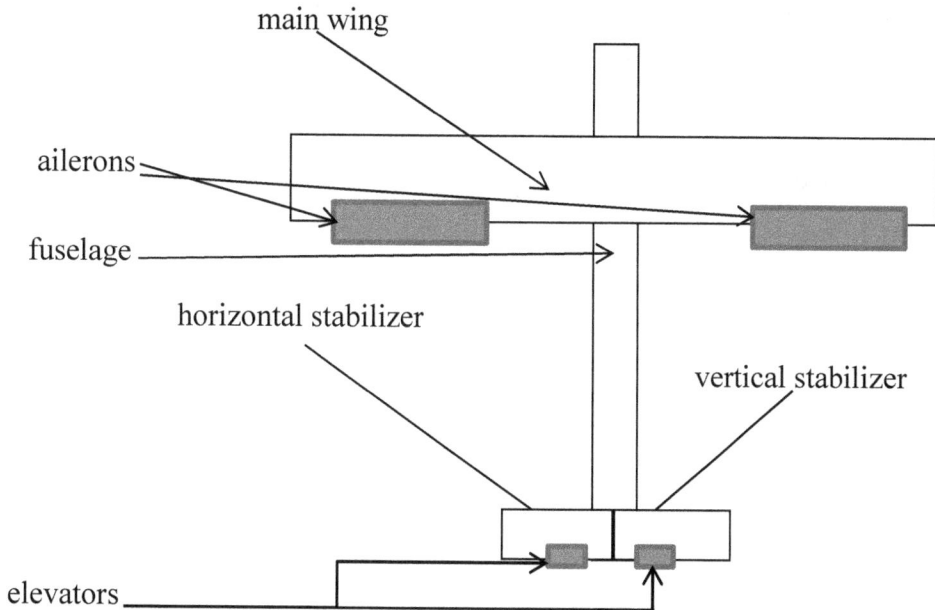

main wing
ailerons
fuselage
horizontal stabilizer
vertical stabilizer
elevators

FIG. 4.2

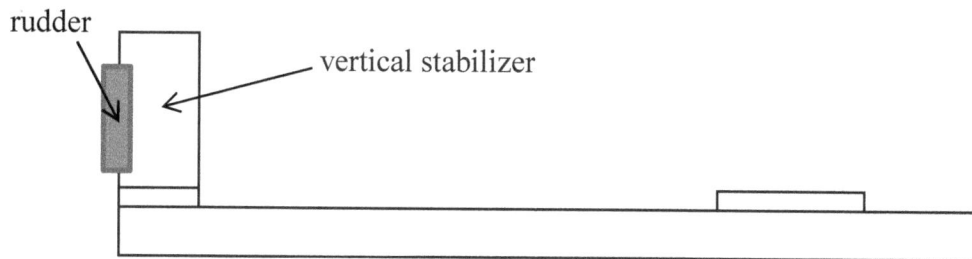

rudder
vertical stabilizer

FIG. 4.3

MATERIALS

1 piece 20 cm × 1 cm × 0.5 cm basswood for fuselage
1 piece 22 cm × 4 cm × 0.2 cm balsa wood
1 piece 10 cm × 2.5 cm × 0.2 cm balsa wood
1 piece 6 cm × 2.5 cm × 0.2 cm balsa wood
7 cm of 2-way tape (floral tape is good)
1-5 g of plasticine

CONSTRUCTION

1. Stick tail onto rear wing using a piece of 2-way tape.
2. Stick rear wing onto fuselage flush with the back of it.
3. Stick main wing onto fuselage (1 to 3 cm from the front of the fuselage).
4. Test fly the plane with the front up slightly before release (Don't throw it too hard.).

1. If the plane dives into the ground, it is nose heavy. Carefully remove the main wing with its tape and move it 1 cm back on the fuselage from its current position.
2. If the plane climbs then falls tail first, it is tail heavy. Take a little of the plasticine and attach it onto the nose (front) of the fuselage.
3. Continue steps 1 or 2 until the plane gradually glides to the floor. It may take a few tries before the plane is balanced.

Extension – Once level flight has been achieved, glue the pieces together using wood glue, and then try the following:

1. Bend the 40 lb. card stock that measures 5 cm × 2 cm lengthwise and tape one piece to within 0.5 cm from the wing's tip on the left and onto the back of the main wing. Do the same on the right side of the wing, but have the aileron facing down; since the left one is up, the plane will roll to the left.
2. Tape 2 pieces of the card stock that measure 2 cm × 1 cm on the back of the rear wing on each side of the tail. These are the elevators. They control the pitch of the airplane (its ability to go up and down).
3. Tape 1 piece of card stock 3 cm × 1 cm to the tail. This is the rudder. It controls the yaw of the airplane (its ability to go left or right).

Chapter 5 – Delta Wing Glider
Designed by Stan Taylor
May 2009

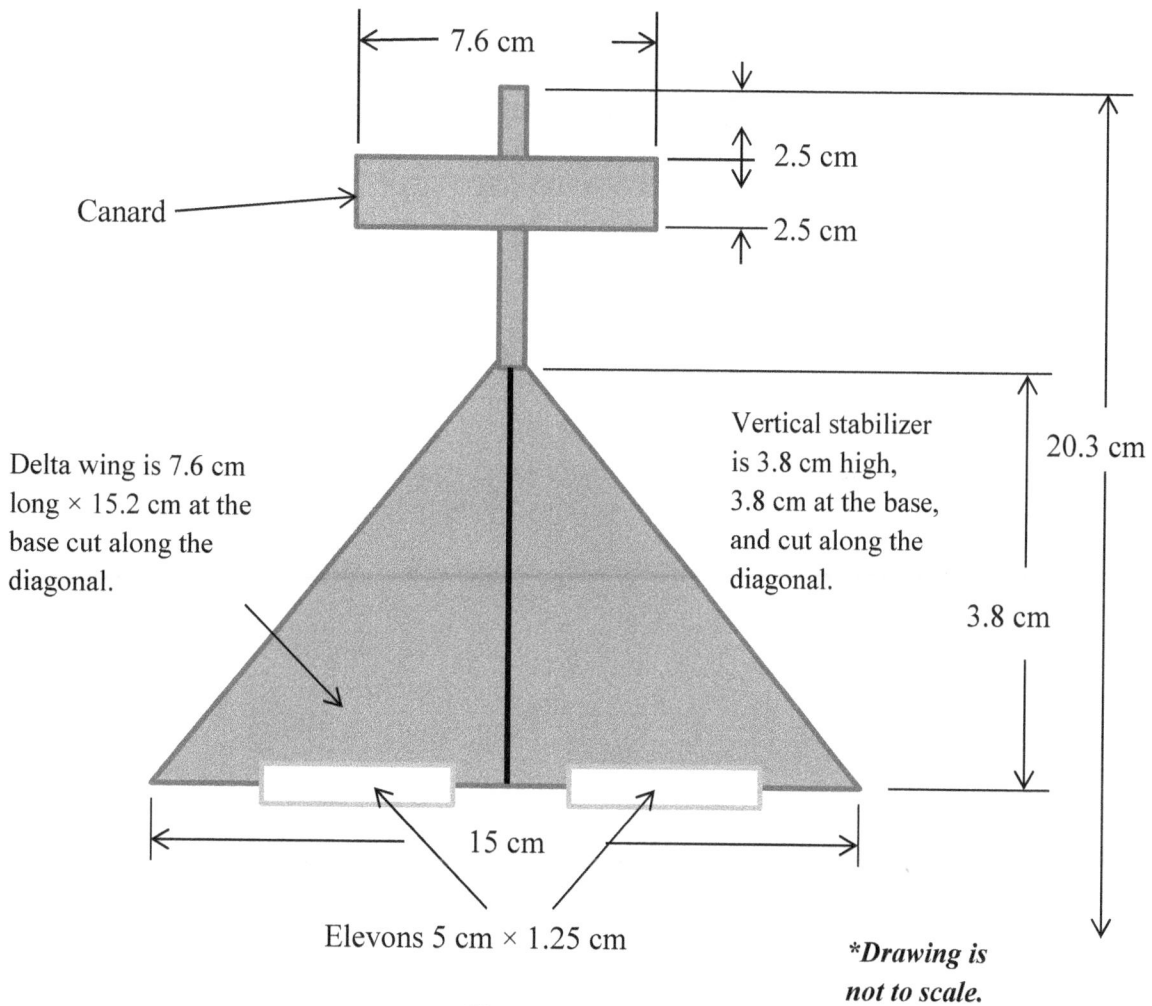

← 7.6 cm →

2.5 cm

Canard

2.5 cm

Delta wing is 7.6 cm long × 15.2 cm at the base cut along the diagonal.

Vertical stabilizer is 3.8 cm high, 3.8 cm at the base, and cut along the diagonal.

20.3 cm

3.8 cm

15 cm

Elevons 5 cm × 1.25 cm

Drawing is not to scale.

FIG. 5.1

NOTE: For the delta wing glider, I use 1/8" (31 mm) balsa for the wing and the canard. With the increase in thickness, the delta wing and other balsa wood planes had to be cut on a bandsaw or a handheld coping saw. I use bass wood for the fuselage because it is sturdier than balsa wood.

See Appendix B for AVRO Arrow design.

FIG. 5.2

EVALUATION:

Design of Balsa Wood Glider

Level 1: demonstrates limited understanding of the design process
Level 2: demonstrates some understanding of the design process
Level 3: demonstrates limited considerable of the design process
Level 4: demonstrates thorough understanding of the design process

Construction of Balsa Wood Glider

Level 1: demonstrates limited skill of the design process
Level 2: demonstrates some skill of the design process
Level 3: demonstrates considerable skill of the design process
Level 4: demonstrates thorough skill of the design process

Flight of the Balsa Wood Glider

Category: Transfer of knowledge and skills (e.g., how to throw the glider; safe use of the equipment; ability to control roll, pitch, and yaw of the glider)

Level 1: transfers knowledge and skills to the flight of the glider with limited effectiveness
Level 2: transfers knowledge and skills to the flight of the glider with some effectiveness
Level 3: transfers knowledge and skills to the flight of the glider with considerable effectiveness
Level 4: transfers knowledge and skills to the glider flight with a high degree of effectiveness

Students' own design – transfer of knowledge and skill to a new design

Level 1: transfers knowledge and skill to a new design with limited effectiveness
Level 2: transfers knowledge and skill to a new design with some effectiveness
Level 3: transfers knowledge and skill to a new design with considerable effectiveness
Level 4: transfers knowledge and skill to a new design with a high degree of effectiveness

Repeat Construction and Flight Evaluations for students' own designed glider.

Chapter 6 – Different Wing Configurations

Try making planes with different wing configurations.

1)   swept back

FIG. 6.1A

USA F-86 Saber Jet Swept Back Wing (https://en.wikipedia.org/wiki/North_American_F-86_Sabre)

FIG. 6.1B

2)   swept forward

canard

FIG. 6.2A

USA X-29 Swept Forward Wing with Canard (https://en.wikipedia.org/wiki/Grumman_X-29)

FIG. 6.2B

3)   dihedral

Boeing 787 Dreamliner (CC BY-SA 3.0, (https://commons.wikimedia.org/w/index.php?curid=207921)

FIG. 6.3A

FIG. 6.3B

4)   anhedral

RAF Harrier (https://en.wikipedia.org/wiki/Dihedral_(aeronautics)

FIG. 6.3A

FIG. 6.3B

To create a dihedral, fill a shallow bowl full of water. Place the wing across the bowl. Put a weight on the middle of the wing (like a bar of sealed plasticine) until the middle of the wing is under water. Leave for 24 hours. Carefully remove the wing from the water, stand it on end, and let it dry for 24 hours. Also try different shaped wings like elliptical, diamond, pointed tips, etc. See Appendix B for AVRO Arrow design and Chinese Chengdu J-10.

Chapter 7 – Flying the Students' Gliders in the Classroom According to the Teacher's Instructions

SAFETY: Do not randomly throw your glider without my supervision. We don't want to accidentally injure a colleague.

Flight 1:

1. Line the students up along one side of the room. Call the first 10 to the front of the room and have them stand beside each other.

2. Advise them to have the nose face up at about a 300° angle for ANGLE OF ATTACK.

3. I will then say, "3-2-1-throw."

4. Have them OBSERVE the flight of their airplane. If it

    a) dives into the floor, it is nose heavy. Have them carefully pull the main wing off the fuselage and move it back 0.5 cm.

    b) goes up immediately, it is tail heavy. Take a little plasticine and put it on the nose of the plane. Later, after the desired amount of plasticine is added, they will place duct tape over the plasticine to hold it in place.

5. Repeat steps 1 to 4 with the next group of 10 until all students get to fly their planes once and make adjustments following Flight 1.

6. Flight 2: Everybody gets to fly their plane a second time and observe what happens.

7. Flight 3: The planes should fly level, (after they've made the necessary corrections) and their planes should gradually descend to the floor.

8. Now it is time to add a few other parts to their plane.

    a) Ailerons: attach them near the wing tip of the main wings using Scotch tape. Students should now conduct Flight 4 and observe roll.

    b) Elevators: attach them to the horizontal stabilizer and close to the vertical stabilizer (0.5 cm) to control pitch. Bend both elevators up. Students should now conduct Flight 5 and observe climb or somersault.

    c) Rudder: attach this to the vertical stabilizer to control yaw. Bend the rudder to the right. Students should now conduct Flight 6 and observe movement to the right.

9. Depending on your budget, have each student build one of the alternate designs listed on page 26.

Chapter 8 – My Adopted Theory of Airplane Lift

When I started teaching "Air and Flight" using the Ontario Curriculum in 1998, I was not comfortable with claims made about airplane lift being attributed to Bernoulli. Bernoulli died before the first balloon flight by two Frenchman and long before airplane flight. Over the years, I read everything I could get my hands on about lift. During the summer of 2006, I read all of the available published documents from NACA (preNASA).

As a plane flies, a number of things are happening as air flows over the wing. Let's break the air down into streamlines for our explanation. Streamline #1 (see diagram below) hits the front top of the wing and wants to go in a straight line (Newton's 1st Law). Fluids don't form voids, so the airstream bends and sticks to the surface of the wing. The bending of the air lowers the pressure. This lower pressure (action) speeds up the air above the wing (reaction) in increasing speed starting with streamline 2 and upward until we hit the free stream of air (the undisturbed air above the wing). The air goes off the trailing edge of the wing much faster than any air from the bottom of the wing. The air going off the trailing edge goes down at the angle of attack of the wing, in the rest frame, according to the pilot. For a person on the ground, in the rest frame, the air appears to be going straight down (presuming you could see the air). Air going down is the action and wing going up is the reaction (Newton's 3rd Law). This, quite simply, is how planes obtain lift.

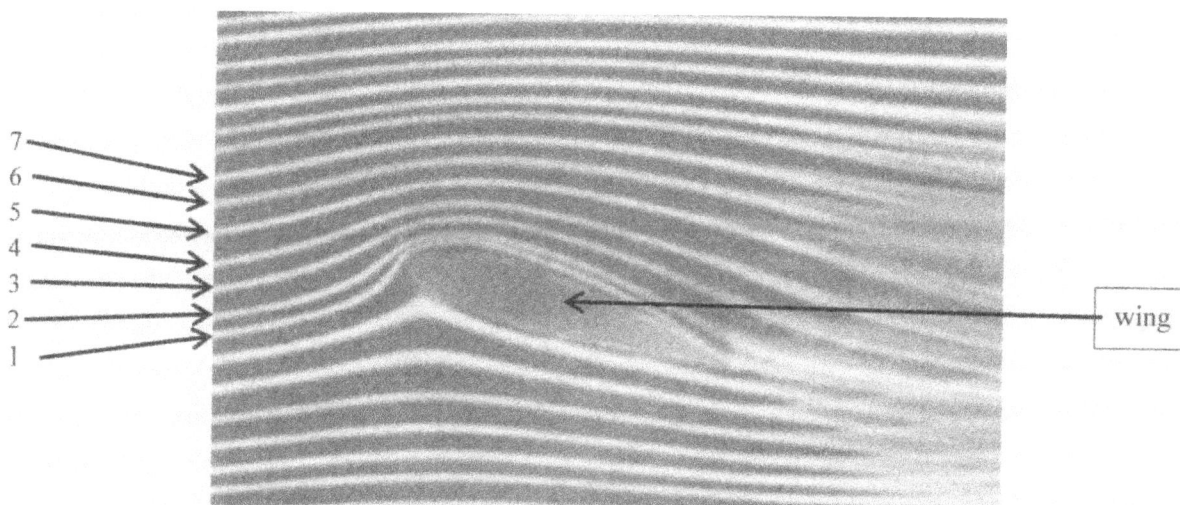

FIG. 8.1

VOCABULARY

Laminar flow is the smooth flow over the wing with no turbulence.

A streamline is a path traced out by a massless particle moving with the flow.

See http://www.cam.ac.uk/research/news/how-wings-really-work for a video that explains air flow and debunks equal transit times.

See http://iopscience.iop.org/article/10.1088/00319120/38/6/001/pdf;jsessionid=EC34CDCE81D 7CA3C93BCA980C537CABE.c1 for a detailed written explanation of lift.

For a more detailed explanation of my adopted view of lift, see David Anderson's and Scott Eberhardt's *Understanding Flight*. Both men are private pilots. In this book they explain that it is the bending of the air stream, viscosity, and the boundary layer that keep the air bent over the curvature of the wing producing downwash off the trailing edge of the wing resulting in lift (Newton's 3rd Law). They explain that without these phenomena flight is not possible.

References

Anderson, D, & Eberhardt, S. (2010). *Understanding Flight* (2nd ed.). New York, NY: McGraw
Hill.

Lagewiesche, W. (1990). *Stick and Rudder.* New York, NY: McGraw-Hill, Inc.

University of Cambridge. (2012, January 25). How wings really work: Airflow across a wing.
Retrieved from http://www.cam.ac.uk/research/news/how-wings-really-work.

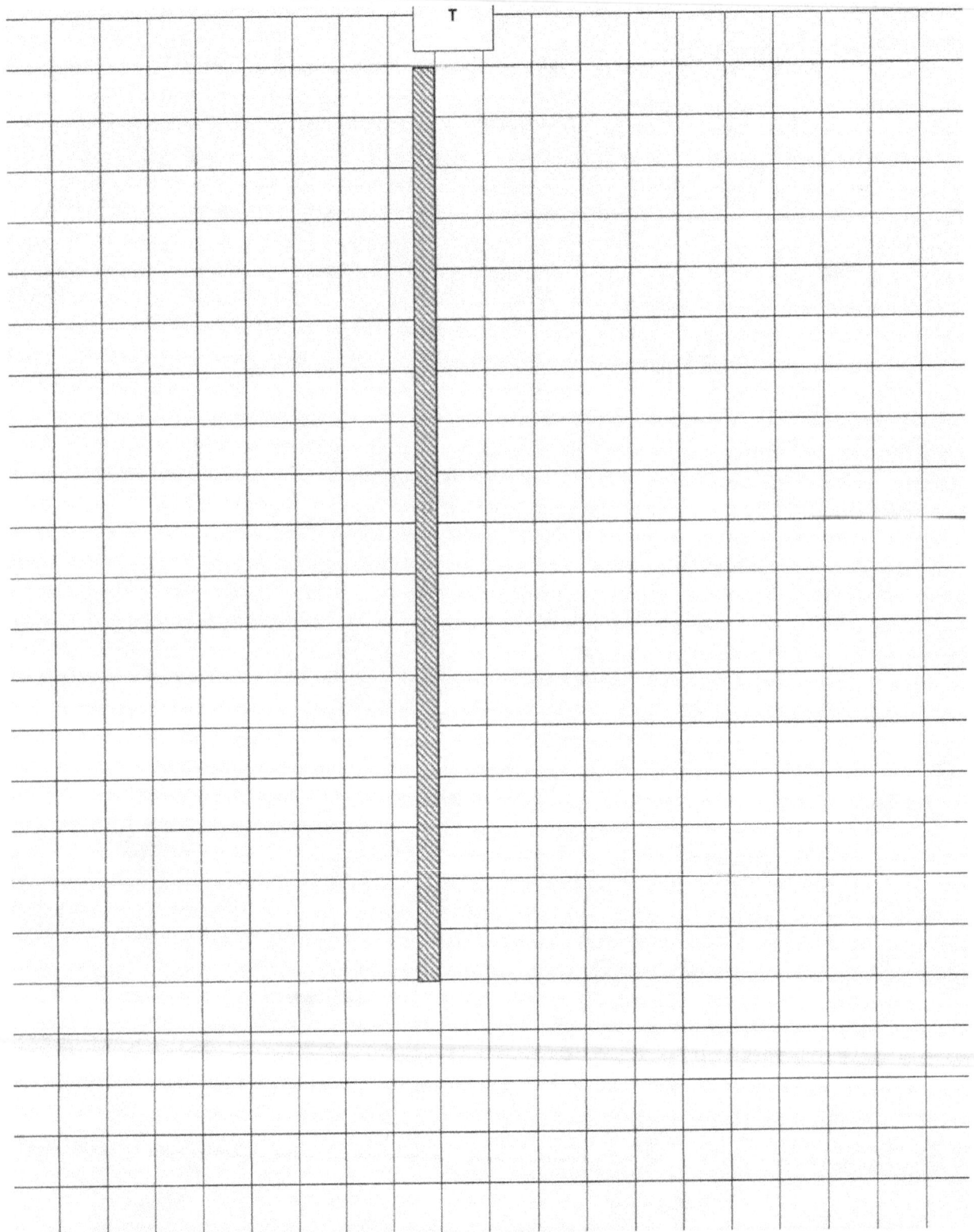

Appendix A

T

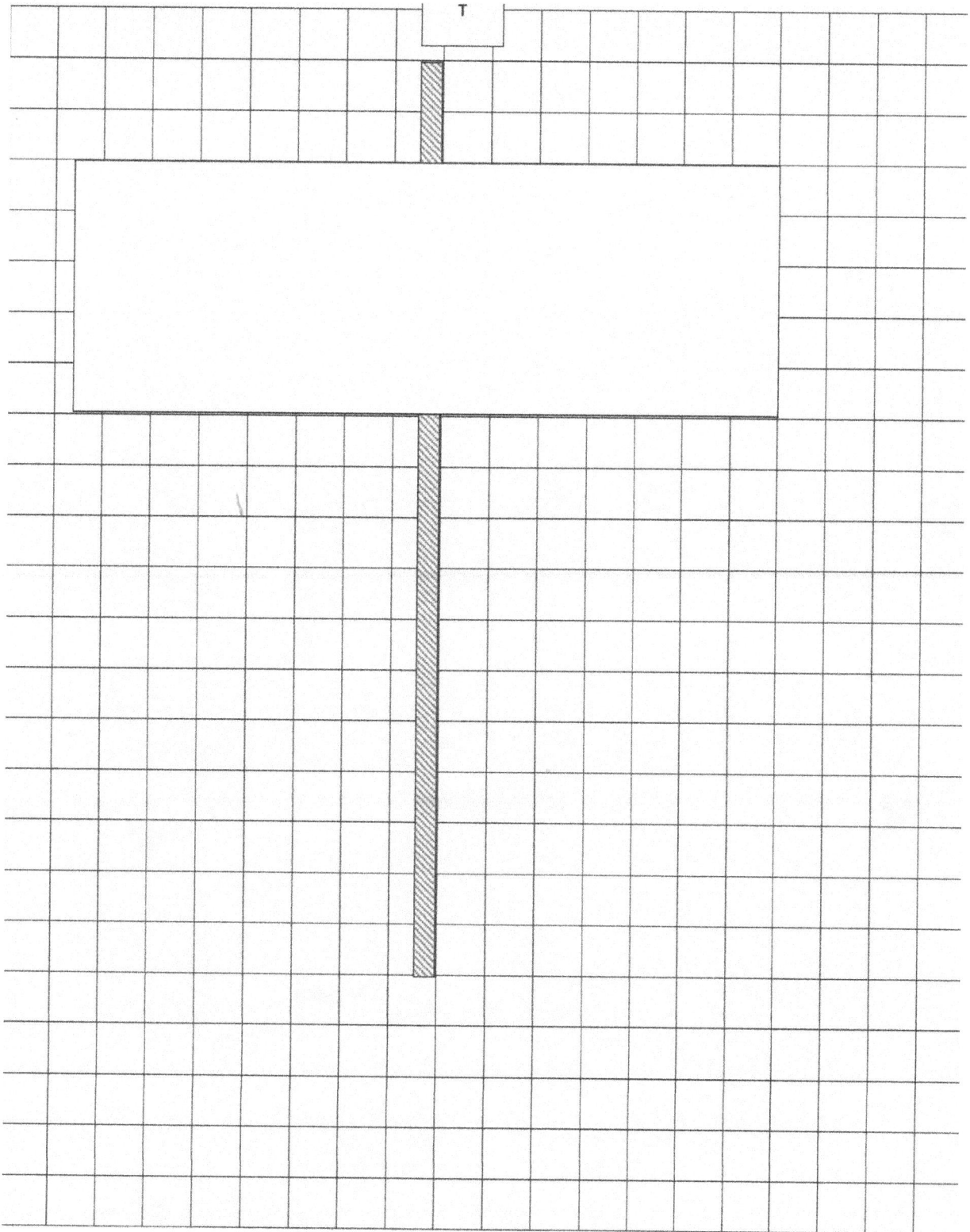

T

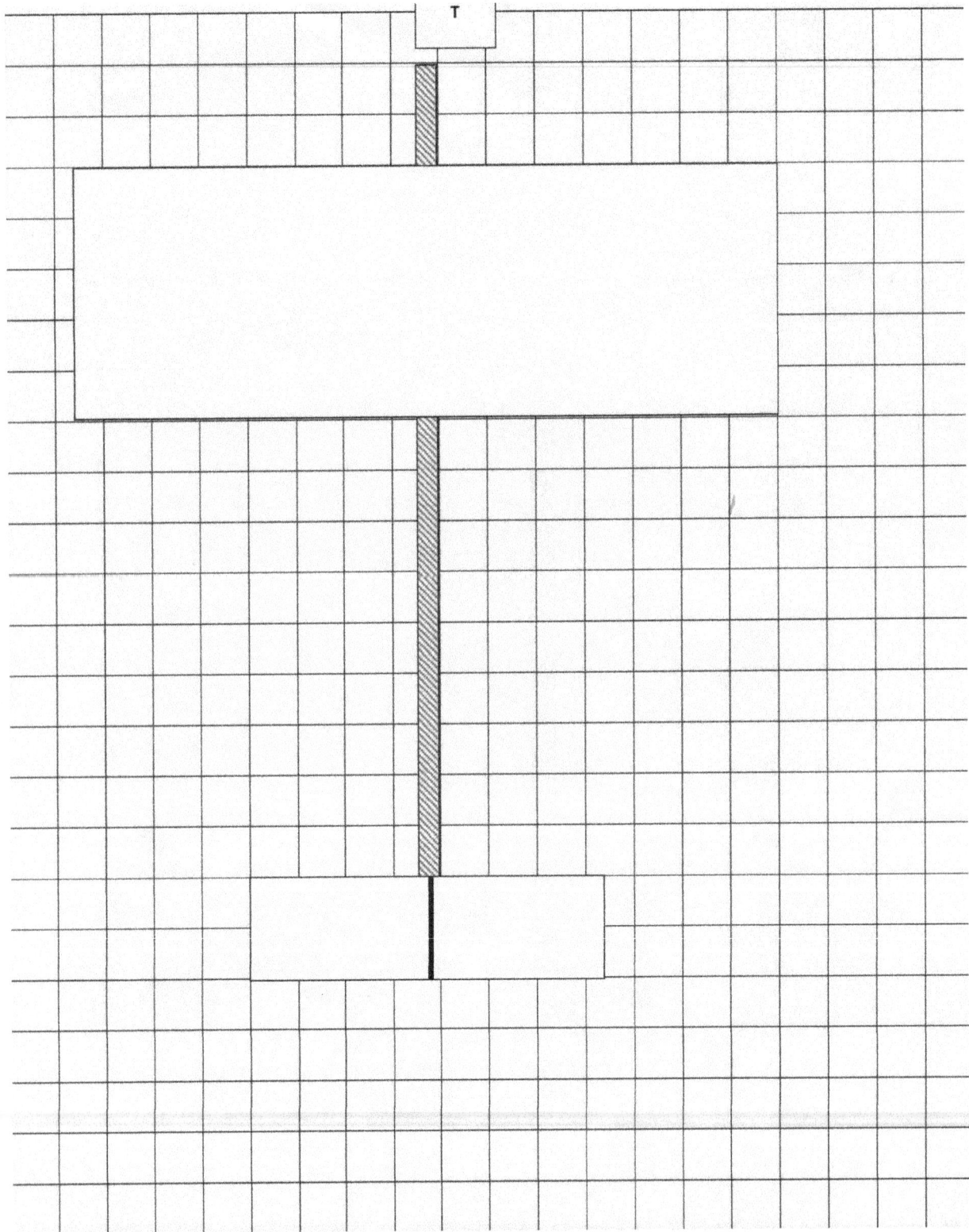

T

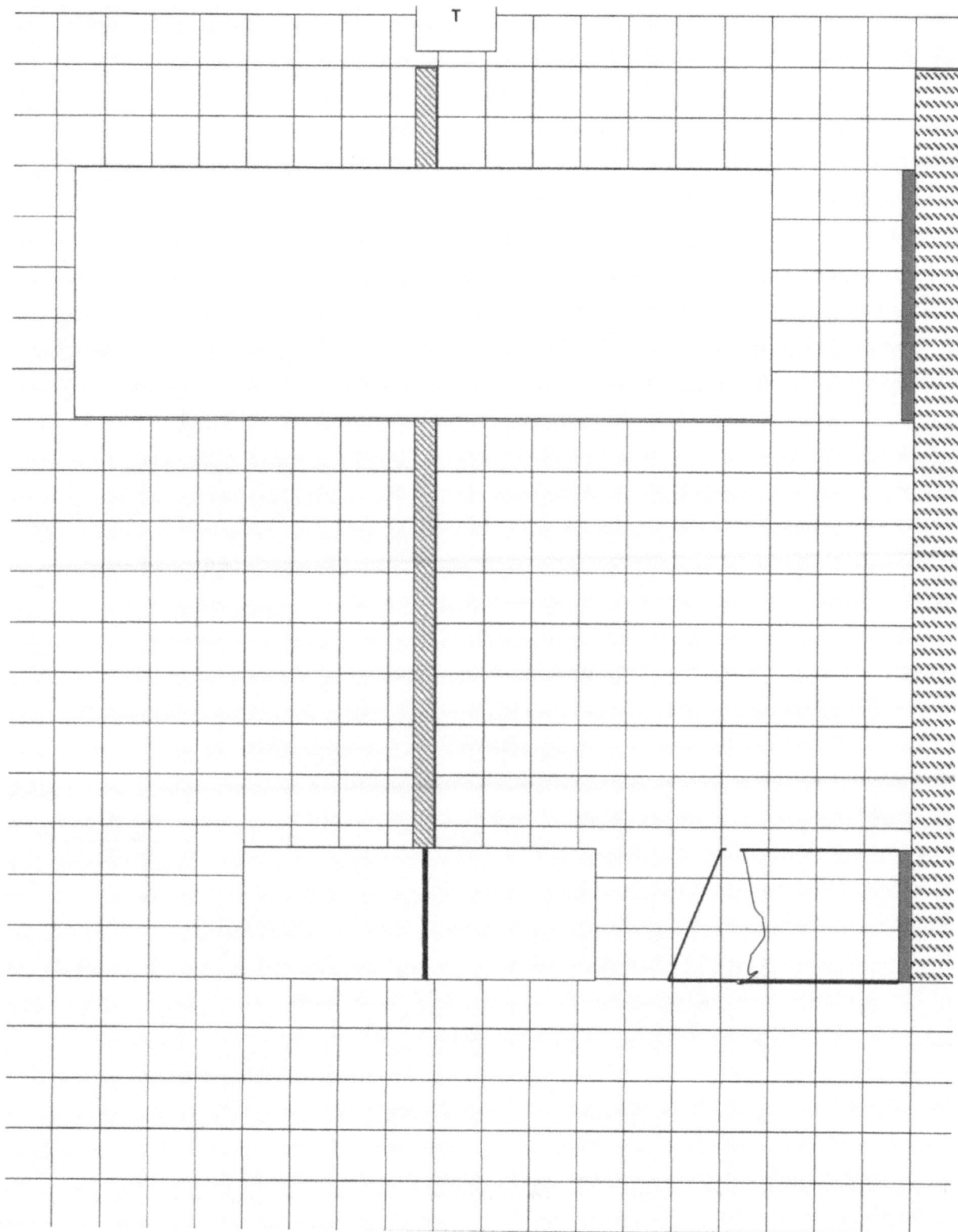

T

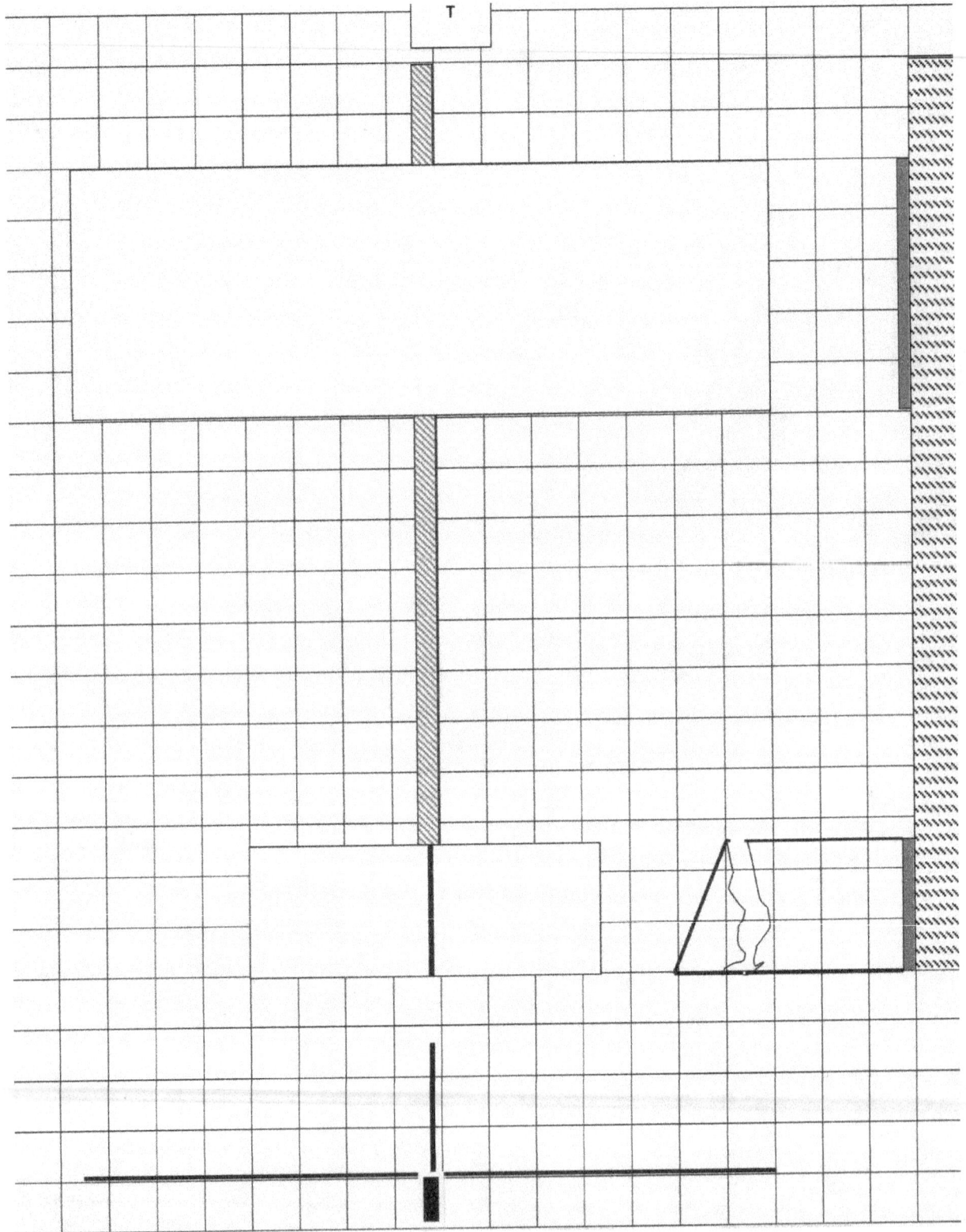

T

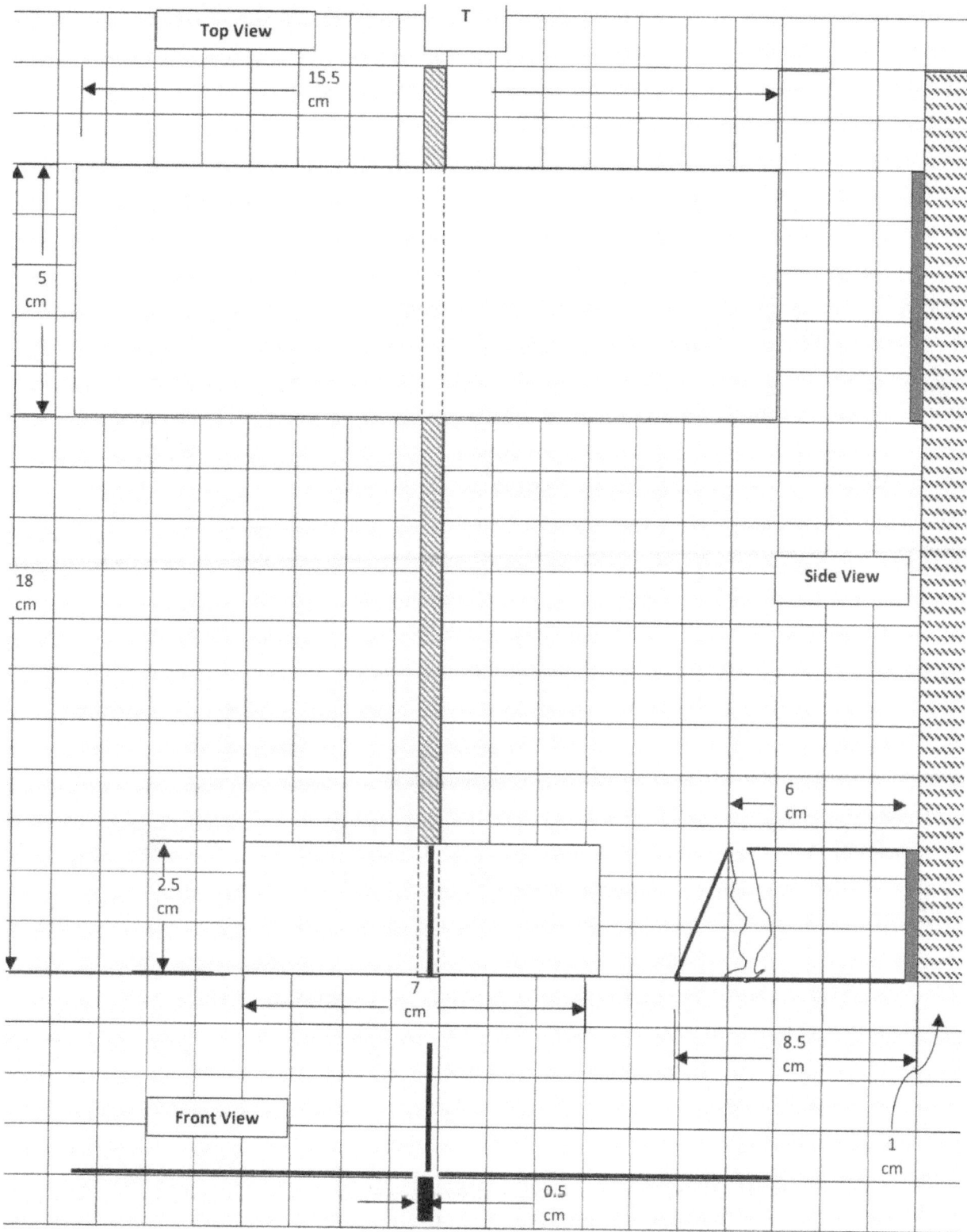

Top View

T

15.5 cm

5 cm

18 cm

Side View

6 cm

2.5 cm

7 cm

8.5 cm

Front View

1 cm

0.5 cm

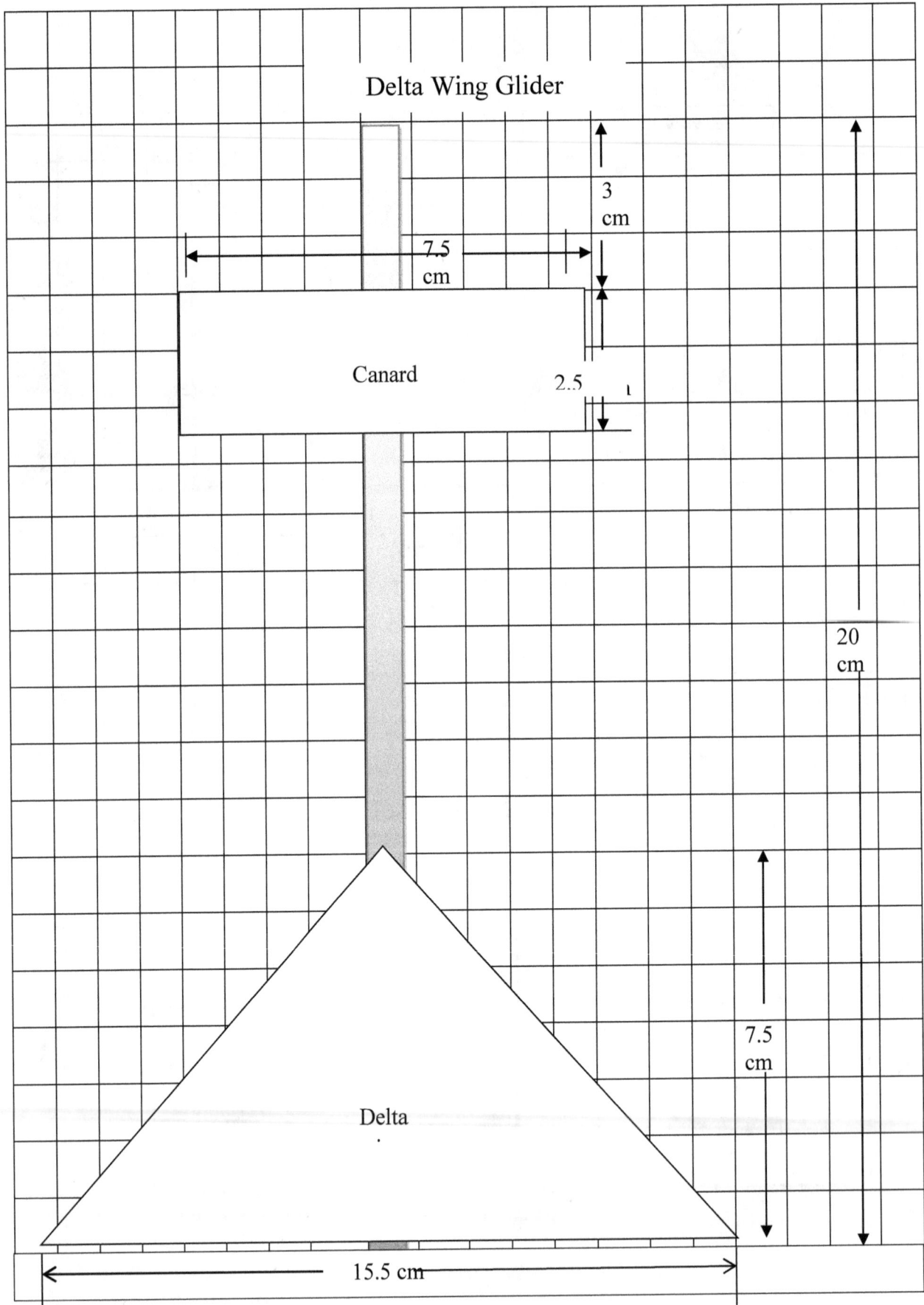

Delta Wing Glider

Canard

3 cm

7.5 cm

2.5

20 cm

7.5 cm

Delta

15.5 cm

Appendix B

Without the canard, and if you used a larger delta wing, you could say it is similar to the AVRO Arrow.

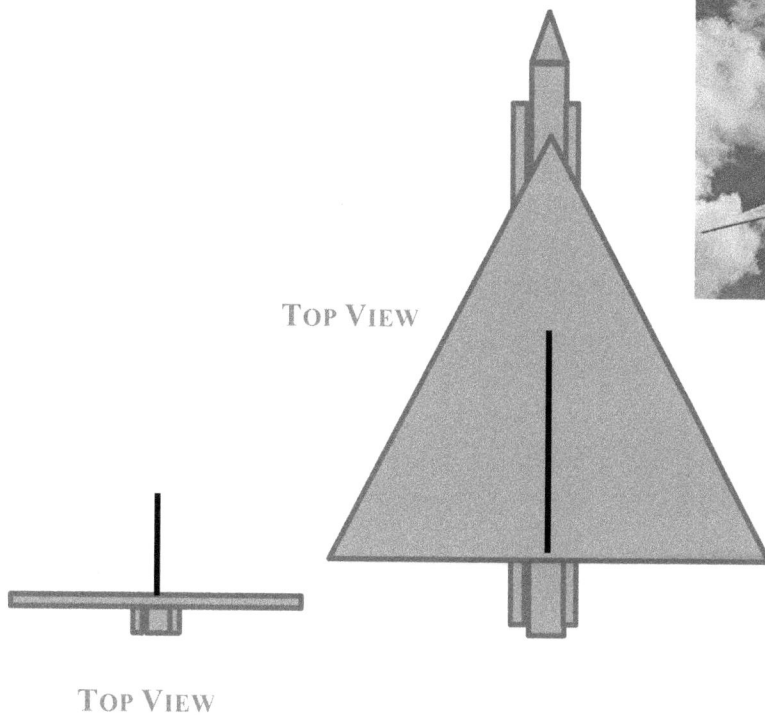

TOP VIEW

TOP VIEW

Photo by Dennis Jarvis - Flickr: DSC_6934 - Canadian Pride, CC BY-SA 2.0, and (https://commons.wikimedia.org/w/index.php?curid=13276285)

If you attach a canard to a delta wing plane, it could be a Chinese Chengdu J-10.

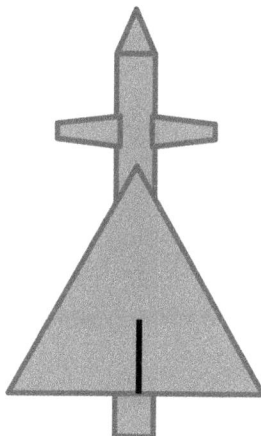

Chengdu J-10 (www.speedgalore.com)

Acknowledgements

I appreciate the emails shared between myself and David F. Anderson. David has explained to me his theory of flight, which I have adopted.

Jess (Jessica) is my granddaughter. She was kind enough to follow my step-by-step instructions for building the paper towel roll glider.

Photographs of the models of the hovercraft and balsa wood gliders were taken by the author.

Holger Babinsky, Ph.D., aeronautical engineer and professor at the University of Cambridge, gave me permission to use the picture shown in this book as Fig. 8.1 following an email discussion. I numbered the streamlines to make it easier for the reader to understand.

See http://www.cam.ac.uk/research/news/how-wings-really-work.

Let the building, and the fun, begin.

Stanley R. Taylor August 2017

About the Author

Stanley R. Taylor taught for the Toronto Catholic District School Board for 23 years. He retired in 2001 and started doing workshops for students, educators, and within the community for Scientists in School (www.scientistsinschool.ca). Stan currently gives science workshops in "Celestial Sleuths" (astronomy) with Grade 6 students and "Structures" with Grades 5 and 3 students. He has given workshops in "Air and Flight" for Grade 6 and "Fluids" for Grade 8.

Not only has Stan conducted workshops for children, but he has delivered workshops for educators at the Science Teachers' Association of Ontario (STAO/APSO) Annual Conference, the Science Exploration Educators' Conference at Johnson Space Center (NASA), the Ontario Association of Physics Teachers Annual Conference, and the Royal Astronomical Society of Canada Annual General Meeting.

Stan has published articles in *Crucible* and *Elements* (the two e-journals of STAO), the *Uxbridge COSMOS,* where he wrote a monthly astronomy column, the *Fredericton Gleaner*, *Canadian Teacher*, and *Metro Voice.*

His published books are *Taylor's Pneumatic Toys* (2012) and *Career Options Maria Sirdar-Nickel* (2015).

Stan is a member of the following organizations:

Retired Teachers Association of Ontario
Professional Writers Association of Canada
Writers Community of Durham Region
Montreal Press Club
Science Teachers' Association of Ontario (STAO)
York Region Astronomy Association
Royal Astronomical Society of Canada (Toronto Center)
Uxbridge an Area Networking Group
Uxbridge Toastmasters
Scientists in School

Find Stan at stanscienceman747@gmail.com, stanscienceman.blogspot.ca, http://stanleyrtaylorcommunications.blogspot.com, http://ca.linkedin.com/pub/stan-taylor/1b/807/2a0, and http://twitter.com/#!/startraveller.